CHEMISTRY IN EVERYDAY LIFE

Industrial Chemicals & Glass Science

Dr. Jeyaraj Prabhu

Dr. Raju Nandhakumar

Preface

Chemicals are the unseen building blocks of modern life, silently working behind the scenes to make our daily lives more comfortable, convenient, and connected. From the moment we wake up to the sound of our alarm clocks, to the moment we drift off to sleep, industrial chemicals are at work all around us. In this book, we invite you to explore the fascinating world of industrial chemicals and glass science and their impact on our day-to-day lives. We will delve into the stories of the chemicals that make our clothes softer, our food taste better, our homes cleaner, and our gadgets smarter. We will uncover the surprising ways in which industrial chemicals shape our daily routines, from the production of everyday essentials like toothpaste and toilet paper to the level of glass blowing – welding technology. In the pages of this book, we will unravel the fascinating world of history track of everyday chemistry, kitchen, herbal and aroma chemistry exploring the intriguing ingredients, innovative formulations, and cutting-edge technologies. In addition, this book provides a firm foundation in all the principal area of glass blowing techniques. Whether you are a student, a professional, or simply a curious mind, this book invites you to join the journey into the world of industrial chemicals and discover the incredible ways in which they touch, transform, and enrich our lives.

Let us uncover the hidden chemistry of our daily lives, and may the stories of these industrial chemicals inspire us to appreciate the science, technology, and human ingenuity that make our world a better place, one molecule at a time.

Dr. Jeyaraj Prabhu & Dr. Raju Nandhakumar

Contents

Preface   *iii*

1. Everyday Chemistry   **1**

Introduction   1

History Track of Everyday Chemistry   1

    i. Prehistory and Everyday chemistry   2

    ii. Classical Era and Everyday Chemistry   6

    iii. The Middle Ages and Everyday Chemistry   8

    iv. Early Modern Era and Everyday Chemistry (A.D. 1450-A.D. 1750)   9

    v. Modern Era (A.D. 1750-Present)   11

2. Your Kitchen Chemistry   **13**

    1. Essential Chemistry & Enrichment in Kitchen   13

    2. Experiments   13

a. Preparation of Aroma Candles   13

b. Preparation of Homemade Lip Balm
   With Beetroot   30

c. Preparation of Phenyl   32

d. Preparation of Homemade Lotion, Such As Shave
   Cream & Face Creams, for Dry Skin.   40

e. Preparation of Dishwasher Powder   44

f. Laundry Detergents   47

3. Your Herbal Chemistry   **49**

1. Herbal & Excitement in Herbal Life   49

2. Experiments   49

a. Preparation of Homemade Ayurveda
   Tooth Powder   49

b. Preparation of Ayurvedic Mouthwash Recipe   55

C. Traditional Method of Making Amla Oil   57

d. Preparation of Natural Insect Repellent Spray   59

4. Your Aroma Chemistry   **65**

I. Some Essentials and their Details   66

1. Common Essential Oils Shelf Life   66

2. Shelf Life of Common Carrier Oils   66

2. Blending Process 69

   i. Blending details 69

   ii. Dilution Table 70

   iii. Essential Oil Conversions 71

   iv. Diluting by Age Group 72

3. Experiments 72

   A. Body Scrubs 73

   b. Foot Scrub Recipe 76

   c. Balms 77

   d. Bath Bombs 79

   e. Ideas for Aromatherapy Inhalers 81

   f. Roller Bottle Blends 83

   g. Lavender Bath Salts 87

   h. Muscle Balms, Tiger Balm and Slave 89

   i. Room Sprays 91

   j. Wood Furniture Polish 95

5. Glass chemistry in Kitchen 97

   1. Etching & Staining Science 97

   Glass Etching: 97

   Glass Staining: 98

Contents

2. Experiments   99

    a. Glass Etching & Staining Science   99

6. Glass Chemistry in Lab   **101**

    a. Glass Science –Bending Methods   101

    b. Glass Science – Cutting methods   103

    c. Glass Science –Blowing Methods   107

Reference   *111*

List of Figures

Fig. No 1 – Stone Age 2

Fig. No 2 – Danish Bronze Age glass beads traced to Egypt 3

Fig. No 3 – Egyptian Glass Beads 3

Fig. No 4 – Late Bronze Age Glass Production at Qantir-Piramesse, Egypt 4

Fig. No 5 – Bronze Age 4

Fig. No 6 – Glass Making Bronze Age – Egypt. 5

Fig. No 7 – Iron Age 6

Fig. No 8 – Herbal Medicines 7

Fig. No 9 – Herbal Medicines extraction from plants 7

Fig. No 10 – Medieval dyeing ideas 8

Fig. No 11 – Medieval Printing Press 9

Fig. No.12 – First Gun and explosive powders 10

Fig. No 13 – Pillar Candle 16

Fig. No 14 – Tea Candles 17

Fig. No 15 – Floating Candle   *17*

Fig. No 16 – Votive Candle   *18*

Fig. No 17 – Gel Candle   *19*

Fig. No 18 – Container Candle   *20*

Fig. No 19. – Lip balm with beetroot   *31*

Fig. No 20. – Raw - Phenyl   *34*

Fig. No 21. – Lotion shave cream   *41*

Fig. No 22. – Face cream   *42*

Fig. No 23. – Dish wash powder with blue   *45*

Fig. No 24. – Liquid laundry soap   *46*

Fig. No 25. – Liquid laundry soap   *47*

Fig. No 26. – Fabric Softener.   *48*

Fig. No 27. – Ayurvedic Powder   *54*

Fig. No 28. – Ayurvedic Mouthwash   *56*

Fig. No 29. – Amla Oil   *58*

Fig. No 30. –Mosquito repellent Oil (Photos 1 to 4)   *60*

Fig. No 31. – Mosquito repellent spray   *61*

Fig. No 32. – Essential Oil in the colour bottle –
Overview picture   *75*

Fig. No 33. – Cross-section photo of the Essential Oil   *75*

Fig. No 34. –Base Foot Scrub Recipe   *76*

Fig. No 35. –Headache Balm.									78

Fig. No 36. – Bath Bomb									81

Fig. No 37. – Inhaler									82

Fig. No 38. – Overview Roller bottle									87

Fig. No 39. – Lavender bath salts									88

Fig. No 40. – Room Sprayer									95

Fig. No 41. – Wood Furniture polish									96

Fig. No 42. – Etched Glass									98

Fig. No 43. –Stained Glass									99

Fig. No 44. – View of Glass bending.									102

Fig. No 45. – Glass cutting view									103

Fig. No 46. – Scoring and hand pressure method									104

Fig. No 47. – Modern portable Glass Cutter									105

Fig. No 48 – Automatic class cutter machine									107

Fig. No 49 – A & B. First Steps in Blowing A Glass Bulb									109

Fig. 49. A – Drawing out the tube.									109

Fig. 49 B – Forming glass rings on the tube									109

Fig. No 49 C – Making A Thick Ring Of Glass									109

Fig. No 49 D – Last Step in Blowing A Glass Bulb									110

Chapter I

Everyday Chemistry

Introduction

Everyday Chemistry is a wonder Science. This wonder can be achieved or attained or modified, recreate the compounds which can be converted into products if the chemistry principles and laws are correctly followed and precisely done the process in any labs or industry. 'Everyday Chemistry' talks about the glasses, candles, sanitiser making, Paints, Herbal medicines, Perfumery items, preparations and processes at home in our daily life.

This book describes Kitchen Chemistry, Modern Day chemistry, Herbal Chemistry, Aroma Chemistry, Glass chemistry in Kitchen and Lab and Business Ladder...

History Track of Everyday Chemistry

This Everyday chemistry is part of our daily life. In the world, no one can skip or avoid this chemistry. It has been used by our ancestors in different domain across the world. Specifically, this chemistry is used in 5 different histories: Prehistory, Classical, Middle Ages, Early Modern, and Modern Eras.

i. Prehistory and Everyday chemistry

The Prehistoric era and Everyday chemistry are tied together like triple ropes. The triple ropes are following.

The First Rope   –   In the Stone Age (2.5 million B.C. to 3000 B.C.)

The Second Rope   –   The Bronze Age (3000 B.C. to 1300 B.C.)

The Third rope   –   The Iron Age (1300 B.C. to 600 B.C.)

Fig. No 1 – Stone Age

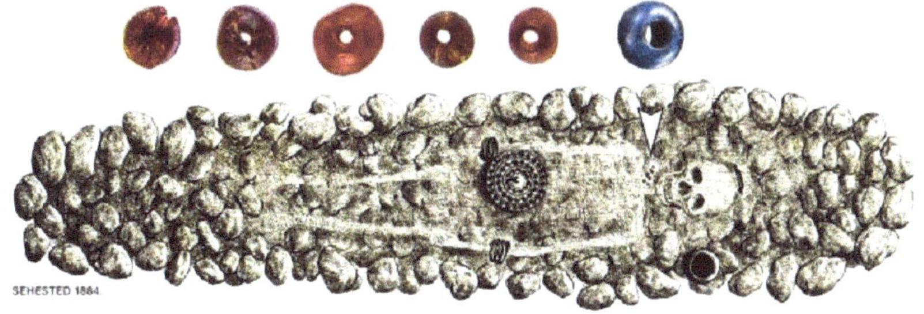

Fig. No 2 – Danish Bronze Age glass beads traced to Egypt

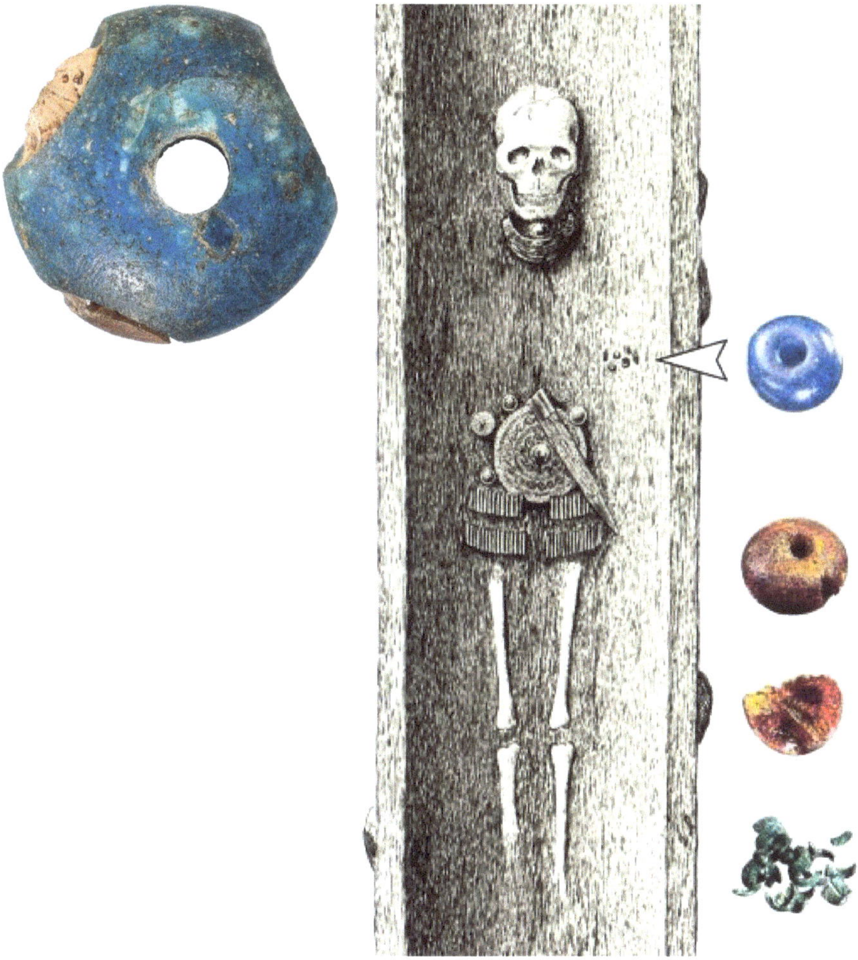

Fig. No 3 – Egyptian Glass Beads

Fig. No 4 – Late Bronze Age Glass Production at Qantir-Piramesse, Egypt

Fig. No 5 – Bronze Age

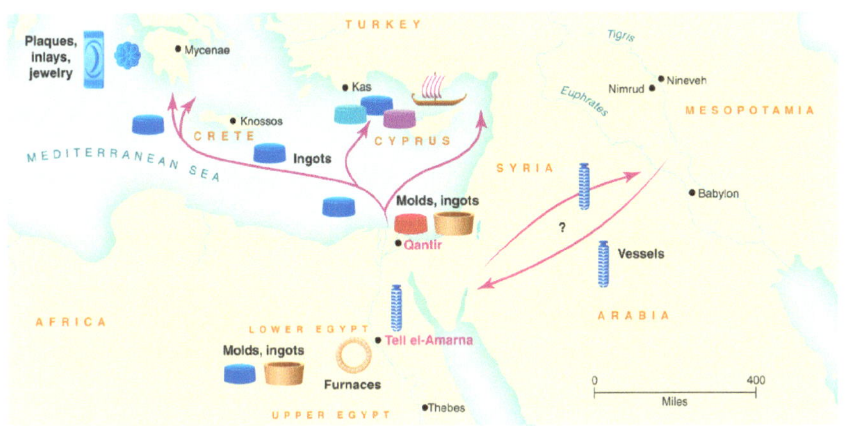

Fig. No 6 – Glass Making Bronze Age – Egypt.

Fig. No 7 – Iron Age

In each and every age or rope, the early humans (Neanderthals, Denisovans) used different stones and created fire (The first chemical reaction), invented the wheel and metal patterns, and introduced ironworks, steel, and writing systems. In further ages, Everyday chemistry is used in all ages in different formats and patterns.

ii. Classical Era and Everyday Chemistry

The classical era includes Ancient Greek, Ancient Rome, Ancient Persian, Byzantine, and Iron Age. different every day herbal medicines were developed by the people.

Fig. No 8 – Herbal Medicines

Fig. No 9 – Herbal Medicines extraction from plants

iii. The Middle Ages and Everyday Chemistry

Many glassware products were developed during the Middle Ages. The glasses were blown and it was turned into articles, decorative items in the early (A.D. 476 to A.D. 1000) and High Middle Ages (A.D. 1000 to A.D. 1250). These glasses were used in the King's Palace and Catholic churches. In the late Middle Ages (A.D. 1250 to A.D. 1450), colour glasses printing machine and dyes were invented.

Fig. No 10 – Medieval dyeing ideas

Fig. No 11 – Medieval Printing Press

iv. Early Modern Era and Everyday Chemistry (A.D. 1450-A.D. 1750)

More metallurgy labs were developed by humans in this era. Practical attempts were done by the early chemists to improve the refining of ores and their extraction to smelt metals. Further, it was introduced in the frontline wars in history. In the following different periods, different war metal heads were developed. In every ore preparation and refining process everyday chemistry is involved.

1. Renaissance Humanism (A.D. 1400 to A.D. 1500)

2. Protestant Reformation (A.D. 1517 to A.D. 1648)

3. The European Renaissance (A.D. 1450 to A.D. 1600)

4. The Enlightenment (A.D. 1650 to A.D. 1800)

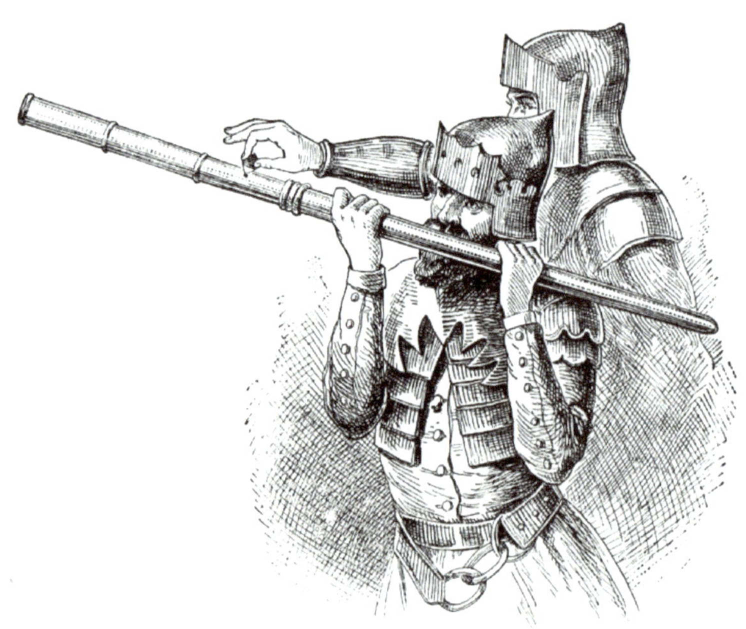

Fig. No.12 – First Gun and explosive powders

v. Modern Era (A.D. 1750-Present)

The influences of both the Renaissance and the Enlightenment led to a technological boom in the Modern era, also known as the Late Modern era. The world of politics was rocked by wars, revolutions and the end of the monarchy in many countries. The Modern era is truly a cumulation of millions of years of human development. In this Era, many household products, kitchen chemistry products, herbal products, and Quarz glasses were developed....

Chapter II

Your Kitchen Chemistry

1. Essential Chemistry & Enrichment in Kitchen

There are many items that are needed at our homes. People are buying every day for their daily life. But many times purchased products are not genuine and trustworthy. Many duplicate, subsided products are in the market. This chapter gives a guideline and reference to prepare such kitchen and toiletry items at our home in a simple process and experiments.

2. Experiments

The following items can be prepared…

a. Preparation of Aroma Candles

Aim:

Preparation of aroma colour candles.

Ingredients:

Wax, double boiler, water, thermometer, wick (thread), desired fragrance oils, moulding blocks or small glass containers, desired pigments, spatula, and sticks.

Procedures:

Using your double boiler, melt the wax. Put a good amount of water in the bottom pan, put about half a pound of wax in the double boiler (this makes the perfect amount to fit in an 8oz mason jar), and watch it melt. It's actually pretty fun to watch. Stir it and break up big chunks with the spatula. It only takes 10-15 minutes for the wax to melt. Be sure to keep an eye on the temperature; you want it to generally be between 160 and 170 degrees. If it gets higher than that, take it off the heat.

While the wax is melting, adhere the wick to the container. Some wicks have a little sticker built-in on the bottom, but most do not. Super glue is one option, but I actually used an old candlemaker's trick with great success: As the wax starts melting, it'll form a pool of liquid. Dip the metal tab of the wick into that melted wax, then quickly adhere it to the bottom of the container — centred, of course. After just a couple of minutes, when the wax hardens, it'll be stuck solid to the bottom.

After all, the wax is completely melted, and you can add your desired fragrance oils. Each wax is different and requires different amounts per pound of wax, so follow the instructions that come with it if you've purchased candle wax specifically. If you bought a block of wax which isn't necessarily just for candles, a safe bet would be 1 oz per pound of wax. Pour the fragrance into your double boiler and stir for 30 seconds or so to ensure it's evenly distributed.

After you've added the fragrance oil, let it cool for a couple of minutes. The optimal temp to pour your wax into the container is around 130-140 degrees; it sets better that way than if poured hotter. This doesn't take very long — just a few minutes — so pay attention to your thermometer.

Once the wax is properly cooled, go ahead and pour it into the container. Keep a light hold on the wick so that it stays in the centre; don't tug too hard, though, or the adhesion to the bottom could be released. Since you're pouring in hot wax, which could melt the wax you used to stick the wick, that could happen anyway. If I gave the wax enough time to harden — 5 minutes or so — it didn't seem to be a problem for me.

Don't pour all the wax just yet, though. Save some in your boiler for after the initial pour sets. You'll notice that it generally gets a nice sinkhole in the centre. We'll come back to that in just a couple of steps.

The wick, while attached to the bottom, may at first do some swaying in the liquid wax. You obviously want to ensure it stays nice and centred while the wax sets and hardens. Having an off-centre wick means it won't burn properly, and you don't want that. Simply place a writing utensil or 2 (ones you don't care a whole lot about) on top of the container with the wick in between. The wick doesn't need to be super secured — it just needs to stay in place for a couple of hours.

As mentioned above, while the wax sets, it'll likely form a sinkhole in the middle. You'll have to let it cool for at least a few hours; it takes that long for the wax to fully set and for you to see how much it needs to be filled in. Re-heat the wax that you left in the boiler and top off the candle. Don't add too much, or you may end up with another hole; just fill in the depression, adding a touch above what was already there for a smooth surface.

You'll probably have a few inches of wick sticking up from your candle. You'll want to trim that down to just about 1/4". A wick that's too long will burn too big and hot. The way to know is by looking at the flame once it's lit: if the flame is more than an inch or so high and flickers a lot, it's too long. Trim it and light it again.

Types of Candles

Type 1 Pillar candle

Fig. No 13 – Pillar Candle

Type 2 Tea-Lights

Fig. No 14 – Tea Candles

Type 3: Floating Candles

Fig. No 15 – Floating Candle

Type 4: Votive Candles

Fig. No 16 – Votive Candle

Type 5: Gel Candle

Fig. No 17 – Gel Candle

Type 06: Container Candles

Fig. No 18 – Container Candle

Benefits :

1. Wax

There are 2 broad categories of candle wax: mineral wax and vegetable wax. Mineral waxes are gotten from paraffin. They are easier to work with and more popular. Vegetable waxes, on the other hand, are natural and are suitable options because they are eco-friendly. Examples of vegetable wax are soy wax, palm wax, coconut wax etc.

- paraffin wax
- beeswax
- soy wax
- palm wax

- coconut wax

- gel wax

- bayberry wax

What is Paraffin Wax?

Paraffin wax is probably what most people think of as 'wax.' This is especially true of those who do not know there are other types. And it is not their fault. Paraffin wax is by far the most popular of all types of wax. It is readily available and very versatile, as it can be used to make container candles and standalone candles (pillar candles). It is gotten from refined crude oil (petroleum). It is odourless and is pale white in colour. It is usually packaged and sold in small slabs and pellet form.

Paraffin Melting Point

Based on their melting points, there are predominantly 2 types of paraffin wax: low melt point wax and high melt point wax. The melting point of the former is less than 130 degrees Fahrenheit. It is suitable for making container candles (using glass jars and tins) and tealight candles. For the latter, its melting point is 130 and 150 degrees Fahrenheit. This type is usually harder and suitable for standalone pillar candles and votives.

Benefits of Paraffin Wax Candles

- Paraffin wax is the most popular type of wax because of its easy availability. They are easy to get both offline and online.

- It is also the cheapest kind of wax. You can compare the prices with other types. Therefore, if you are making your candles on a modest budget, consider paraffin wax.

- Paraffin wax's popularity surely gives it an edge over other types of wax in that there are a lot more resources for it than for other types. Most of the information one will find online is based on paraffin wax. In fact, many candle-making additives (fragrances and dyes) were made with paraffin wax.

- It is very easy to work with. Most people do not need any additional special instructions. As such, it is recommended for candle-making beginners.

- Fragrance and dyes work well with paraffin wax. It holds both very well and disperses fragrance more effectively. One can easily make coloured candles to decorate the home with paraffin wax.

Disadvantages of Paraffin Wax Candles

- It is not natural as it is gotten from refined petroleum.

- Because it is gotten from refined petroleum, this means it is toxic. Paraffin wax is composed of toxic ingredients and pollutes the home. This means it cannot be used by or around people with respiratory problems or certain allergies. This unsafe nature of the wax has made people look for natural alternatives.

- Paraffin wax leaves residue (black soot) around where it is used and this can be unsightly. Candles are mostly meant to be used as decorations. So when you have a wax that stains the containers and other surfaces black, the original purpose of decoration is defeated.

Soy Candle Wax

Paraffin wax has left many worried about its toxic nature. Hence, a lot of people now opt for an all-natural alternative, soy wax. This wax, gotten from soybean oil, is relatively new, only invented in the 1990s.

Soy Wax Melting Point

It has a lower melting point than paraffin wax and other types of candle wax. This means it also burns cooler. Its melting point is about 120 – 180 degrees Fahrenheit. It is a very economical choice as it burns longer than paraffin wax. It is more suitable for making container candles but can be used to make pillar candles too.

Soy wax is sold mostly in pellet form, and its pricing is similar to that of paraffin wax, although the latter is cheaper. Paraffin wax and soy wax are the most popular types of wax. Soy wax also burns cleanly, and it is a good choice for most people, especially those who oppose paraffin wax. Soy wax is also very effective for those who want to blend waxes together. For example, paraffin–soy wax blends have become common. It can also be blended with palm wax.

Benefits of Soy Wax Candles

- It is a completely natural type of wax. This excludes, of course, cases when it is blended with another type of wax, such as paraffin wax.

- It is gotten from soybean oil and can be easily produced in large quantities. This is unlike beeswax, which you will learn about next.

- It is very cheap. This, plus its non-toxic nature, is one of the reasons soy wax is an effective competitor against paraffin wax in the market. They are both about the cheapest kinds of wax you will find.

- It burns evenly and produces little soot.

- When spilt, soy wax can be easily cleaned off surfaces with soap and warm water.

Disadvantages of Soy Wax Candles

- Soy wax has a low melting point. This means candles made with it can easily melt in hot weather.

- It does not throw off fragrances or paraffin wax.

- It needs to be preserved. If not, it will spoil. You have to take note of this. Without preservatives, you should probably only buy soy wax when you are ready to use it.

Beeswax

Beeswax is another type of natural wax, gotten from the honeycombs of bees. It is the oldest known type of wax. Unlike the first 2 types, whose colours are somewhat white, beeswax has a golden colour. This means that there is no real need for dyes to be added; its colour is naturally beautiful. Adding fragrances is also redundant as it also has a natural scent of honey.It also burns bright and clean, with little smoke. Beeswax is one of the best types of wax you will find. Perhaps the best feature of beeswax is its ability to purify the air around the candle instead of polluting it. As it burns, it produces negative ions that draw pollutants from the air around it.

Beeswax Melting Point

Beeswax has a high melting point, around 145 degrees Fahrenheit, and it burns longer.

Benefits of Beeswax Candles

- It is all-natural and does not pollute the air. It purifies it instead. It is eco-friendly.

- Unlike soy wax, beeswax never goes bad. You can keep it at home as long as you like until you are ready to use it.

- Its high melting point means beeswax candles take longer to burn than other types of wax.

- It has a natural scent and a natural golden colour. You have no real need for fragrances and dyes when making your candles with it.

- It burns brightly and produces little smoke.

Disadvantages of Beeswax Candles

- Beeswax is not easy to get. It takes about 5 pounds of honey for bees to produce just one pound of wax. This, in turn, makes it very rare.

- As a result of its rarity, beeswax is also very costly. Though effective, it is the most expensive type of wax. This discourages many from using it.

- It is highly flammable. One needs to be extra careful when working with it and also when using beeswax candles.

Palm Candle Wax

This is another natural type of wax. It is usually gotten from Oil Palm trees. It has a natural yellow-brown colour. It can be used to make either container of pillar candles. It is the hardest of all-natural candles. This means it provides the rigidity necessary for making pillar candles. Also, it can be blended with soy wax for extra hardness while still being all-natural.

Palm Wax Melting Point

Its melting point is around 140 degrees Fahrenheit. This is higher than that of all other natural waxes.

Though priced above paraffin wax, it is not very expensive (far less compared to beeswax). One will usually find it sold in flakes. Candles made with palm wax burn well and last long. Palm wax has been gaining popularity among candle makers in recent times. It can be blended with beeswax; this makes the candle (especially pillar candles) look glossy when ready.

Benefits of Palm Wax Candles

- Being a natural wax, it is very eco-friendly and non-toxic.

- Just like beeswax, its high melting point means it will not melt in hot conditions (unlike soy wax).

- Palm wax is easy to work with. One can easily use it to produce different surface patterns.

Disadvantages of Palm Wax Candles

It is gotten from Oil Palm trees. This means that there is the danger of deforestation in cutting down trees to make different things (including wax).

Gel Candle Wax

Gel Wax is not actually a wax. It is made of mineral oil gotten from paraffin and poly resins. It is a new alternative as it came in only in the 20th century. It is the kind of wax to have fun with. It holds fragrance well and can also be easily decorated. Different materials can be suspended in it for effect and you can also add glitter. Gel wax is particularly beautiful because of its transparent look which is maintained even when you add colour to it.

As it is a very soft kind of wax, it is only suitable for use in container candles. There are varying degrees of density when working with gel wax. The low density does not allow for many scents to be added and is suitable for beginners to use.

Medium-density gel wax is thicker and holds more fragrance. The high-density one allows for a large amount of scent. Gel wax candles burn well and longer. Since today's candles are mostly meant for decoration, gel wax is the ultimate means of fulfilling this purpose.

Benefits of Gel Candles

- Gel wax is fun to work with. You can add a lot of decorative materials that will make your candles a lot more beautiful.

- It provides for a longer burn. It burns for a much longer time than other waxes, such as paraffin and soy. It is an economical choice.

- It is not expensive. This makes it a good option if your budget is small.

Disadvantages of Gel Wax

- Mineral oil gotten from paraffin is part of its composition. This means that, like paraffin wax, it is toxic as it emits air pollutants.

- Gel wax is not very easy to work with, especially for beginners. It takes a lot of practice.

It also burns at a higher temperature. Gel wax has been known to burn so high that the containers explode. One has to be really careful working with gel wax.It is only suitable for use in making container candles and not pillar candles because it is very soft. One needs to be careful when choosing fragrance oils as not all fragrance oils are compatible with gel wax. Learn how to make gel wax.

Coconut Wax

Coconut wax is another natural type of wax and is gotten from coconut oil. What is called coconut wax is a blend of coconut oil with other natural waxes.

Coconut Wax Melting Point

Its melting point is between 75 and 100 degrees Fahrenheit. This low melting point means it will likely melt on its own in hot weather. It burns evenly and slowly. It is also known to throw off scent well. It is also a very eco-friendly type of wax. However, it is only suitable for use in making container candles as it is very soft.

Benefits Of Coconut Wax Candles

- By burning slowly, candles made with coconut wax last longer
- It is an all-natural alternative and very eco-friendly.
- It throws off scent effectively.

Disadvantages of Coconut Wax

- It is very expensive (not as beeswax, though) and hard to get.
- It is not suitable for use in hot weather because of its low melting point.
- It cannot be used to make pillar candles.

Bayberry Wax

This is a natural type of wax, gotten by burning the berries gotten from bayberry bushes. It has a natural green colour and natural scent, too.

Bayberry Wax Melting Point

Its melting point is between 115 to 120 degrees Fahrenheit. However, it is not very easy to get. It takes more than 10 pounds of berries just to make a pound of wax. This contributes to its high cost, which is a turn-off for many. It is hard and has a brittle surface. Its hardness makes it suitable for making both pillar and container candles.

Benefits of Bayberry Candles

- It has a natural scent and colour. This means you are good to go even without additives.

- It can be used to make either pillar or container candles.

Disadvantages of Bayberry Wax

- While bayberry wax is known to be hard, its brittle surface means it can break very easily.

- It is difficult to get and, therefore, very expensive.

All types of candle wax listed above are good choices, depending on what you want (or do not want). You can also work with different types to find the one that suits you best. With this guide, you should not be confused about the type of wax you need for your candles any longer.

b. Preparation of Homemade Lip Balm With Beetroot

Aim:

Prepare Lip balm from vegetables to avoid cracks in the lips during the winter season.

Ingredients:

1 beet
1/2 teaspoon beeswax
1/2 teaspoon shea or cocoa butter
1/2 teaspoon coconut oil

Mandolin or sharp knife
Dehydrator
Coffee grinder
Cheesecloth
Small saucepan
Glass measuring cup or jar.
Lipstick container or tube

Procedure:

- Using a mandolin or sharp knife, slice beet into thin strips and lay it out on the dehydrator screen. Set the dehydrator to 120 degrees, and dehydrate for 6 to 8 hours. (You can try cherries, raspberries, cranberries, or strawberries for different tints of red and pink.)

- Once the beets are thoroughly dried, pulse the chips in a spice grinder until you have a fine powder.

- Bring 1-2 inches of water to a simmer in a small saucepan over low heat. Add beeswax, shea or cocoa butter, and coconut oil to a glass measuring cup or jar and set in water. Stir until completely melted, 5 to 10 minutes. Add 1/2 teaspoon beetroot powder and stir until dissolved. The colour of the lipstick will lighten when it cools. If you find the colour is not dark enough for your liking, add colourant and let the mixture steep for up to an hour.

- Remove from heat and pour through a cheesecloth to strain out any larger gritty particles. Twist fabric to wring out.

- Carefully pour into the lip container, filling until almost overflowing. Let cool for half an hour or until solid.

Fig. No 19. – Lip balm with beetroot

Benefits

1. Beet Root Powder

Beetroot powder is rich in antioxidants, dietary fibre, calcium, iron, potassium, folate, manganese, and other nutrients. Perhaps most remarkably, beets are naturally rich in nitrate, compounds that can improve blood flow and lower blood pressure, leading to notable health benefits. Beet powder, also called beetroot powder, is a similarly bright pink or red product made from dried ground beets. Beet powder is often advertised as a superfood and sold by natural food retailers. Beet powder can be mixed with water to create a juice. It can also be added to smoothies, sauces, or baked goods.

c. Preparation of Phenyl

Aim:

To prepare phenyl (disinfectant) for domestic purposes.

Ingredients:

The following are the raw materials generally used in the manufacture of phenyl. –Rosin, pale yellow to deep brown (black type is not suitable), Caustic soda castor oil (ordinary quality), Light cresote oil containing 25 to 30% carbolic acid.

Procedure: 1

The scope for the manufacture of this disinfectant should be prepared as soft soap. This is first dissolved in water and then the cresote oil is added to form the emulsion. Great care needs to be taken while the saponification of the oil with the alkali takes place. The heat should be regulated very carefully, and it should be seen that the flame does not come into contact with the surface of the oil. The sudden increase in temperature may also be accompanied by swelling up of the mass and the subsequent flowing over, which must be prevented.

Process:

1. Weigh and put the materials separately in different plastic containers

2. Prepare the caustic soda solution. Take the required quantities of resin and castor oil in a pan.

    Then heat the above material till it is dissolved. Add slowly caustic soda solution to the above-dissolved mass. Care is to be taken that in no case the mass overflows the pan. To control this, add caustic soda solution little by little. In this way, when the major portion of the caustic soda solution is mixed, the boiling slowly comes down. Now add the remaining caustic soda solution and continue boiling for about 15 minutes.

3. The heating is to be continued till the reaction is completed, which can be determined by adding a few drops to a glass of water when a white solution should result.

4. Now mix the water and boil. Allow the solution to boil a little by extinguishing the first, then transferring it into a steel drum and mixing the light creosote oil. Close these of the drums and keep them aside to cool for a day when the product is ready for use.

    This Product is a good type of fluid, when a little of this is added to a glass of water, it at once produces a thick milky white emulsion with good odour.

5. Processed in the same way as above.

Fig. No 20. – Raw - Phenyl

Procedure: 2

How to Formulate Black Phenyle Disinfectant

Black phenyle (sometimes written as phenyl) is a dark brown or black liquid that is manufactured as a powerful disinfectant. Black phenyle is most often used in hotels, hospitals, military facilities, homes, and animal farms, among other places. Black phenyle is very powerful and can effectively disinfect even when it is very dilute. For this reason, it is economically beneficial for large facilities to keep a stock of concentrated black phenyle and dilute it with water. Just be sure to wear gloves and goggles when making black phenyle solution, as it can be dangerous.

Method 1

a. Making a Soap Solution

Start with castor oil. Castor oil will be the base solvent for your soap solution. Roughly 90 percent of the soap solution will consist of castor oil. Pour the oil into a container that is safe to heat on the stove top or over a Bunsen burner.

For example, 890 mL of castor oil is used to make 1 L of soap solution.

b. Prepare and Add Rosin.

Rosin is a dry form of pine resin. It is solid and brittle at room temperature but can be melted on the stovetop. Heat the rosin until it is in a liquid form. Roughly 10 percent of your soap solution will be rosin. Pour the rosin into the castor oil. This will give the solution a pine scent.

For example, 90 mL of rosin will be added to 890 millilitres (30.1 oz) of castor oil to make 1 L soap solution.

Rosin is easily found online. You can also find smaller quantities of it at music retailers as it is commonly used for the bows of stringed instruments.

c. Add Caustic Soda

A caustic soda is the common name for a sodium hydroxide (NaOH) solution. NaOH is available online as well as in some specialty craft stores. Make the solution by adding 0.5% NaOH to a given volume of water. You only need to make a small volume of caustic soda solution, as it will only be one to 2 percent of the total soap solution.

In the example of a 1 L solution, you would add 20 millilitres (0.68 fl oz) of caustic soda solution to 890 millilitres (30.1 fl oz) of castor oil and 90 millilitres (3 fl oz) of rosin.

To make 20 millilitres (0.68 fl oz) of caustic soda solution, you would add 0.1 mg of NaOH to 20 millilitres (0.68 fl oz) of water and warm the water slowly while stirring. When the NaOH has completely dissolved, you will have a clear caustic soda solution that is ready to use.

Do not let the caustic soda solution cool before adding it to the soap solution.

d. Heat the mixture

Heat the mixture on the stove or over a Bunsen burner until it develops into a soap. To test the consistency of the solution, you can dip a piece of paper into it. If it leaves an oily stain on the paper, the solution will need to be heated longer.

Method 2

Adding Antimicrobials

Remove the mixture from heat. There is no need to heat the solution when adding the germicidal compounds. Place the mixture on a heat-proof surface (e.g., a granite countertop or into a larger container of sand). Take care not to spill any of the soap solution.

The soap solution will make up 20 percent of your total black phenyle solution.

Add creosote oil. Creosote oil is a source of phenol derivatives, including carbolic acid. These compounds are necessary for the disinfecting properties of black phenyl. Thirteen percent of the black phenyle solution will be creosote oil.

To make a 5 L batch of black phenyl, you will add 650 millilitres (22 fl oz) of creosote oil to 1 L of soap solution. Creosote oil is not a commonly available product. You will need to work with a licensed chemical supplier to get this ingredient.

Use chloroxylenol. Chloroxylenol will boost the germicidal properties of the black phenyle solution. It should comprise 2.5% of the total solution. You can purchase chloroxylenol from lab and manufacturing retailers or online.

For the same 5 L batch of black phenyl, you would add 125 millilitres (4.2 fl oz) of chloroxylenol to 650 millilitres (22 fl oz) of creosote oil and 1 L of soap solution.

Like creosote oil, chloroxylenol isn't available everywhere. You will need to work with a chemical supply company or a medical supply company to procure this ingredient.

Pour into water. Water is the most abundant ingredient in black phenyle disinfectant. The solution contains 64.5% water. Pour the mixture into the water while slowly stirring.

For a 5 L batch of black phenyl, you will add 3.225 L of water to 125 millilitres (4.2 fl oz) of chloroxylenol, 650 mL of creosote oil, and 1 L soap solution.

Method 3

Diluting a Black Phenyle Solution

Pour water into a bucket. By pouring the water first, you avoid the risk of concentrated phenyle solution splashing back on you. You can use hot or cold water. Tap water is acceptable to use.

Pour water into a bucket. By pouring the water first, you avoid the risk of concentrated phenyle solution splashing back on you. You can use hot or cold water. Tap water is acceptable to use.

Add black phenyle solution. One benefit to black phenyle as a disinfectant is that you only need a small amount. A ratio falling between 1:256 and 1:64 black phenyle to water is appropriate. Pour the phenyle into the water. You will only need to add between 4 millilitres (0.14 fl oz) and 15 mL of black phenyle solution to 1 L of water to have the desired disinfecting properties.

Stir the solution. The solution should have a cloudy white colour. After stirring for 10 to 20 seconds, let the solution sit. After approximately 5 minutes, stir the solution again and it is ready to use.

Benefits & information

1. About Rosin

Rosin Uses Rosin is an ingredient in printing inks, varnishes, adhesives (glues), soap, paper sizing, soda, soldering fluxes, and sealing wax. Rosin can be used as a glazing agent in medicines and chewing gum. It is denoted by E number E915. A related glycerol ester (E445) can be used as an emulsifier in soft drinks. Rosin is a cannabis concentrate created via a specific extraction technique that involves no solvents. The process involves the use of heat and pressure to squeeze resinous sap from cannabis flowers. This often results in a very clean-tasting product. Rosin also has a high level of cannabinoids and terpenes, making it a highly sought-after product.

2. Castor oil

The health benefits of castor oil include boosting immunity, skin and hair care, and relieving rheumatism, menstrual disorders, and constipation. It also helps induce labour and improve lactation. Castor oil improves lymphatic function, blood flow, and thymus gland health.

3. Cresote Oil

Creosote essential oil health benefits are great things that come from a bush plant. This oil is a type of oil made from tar; there is also what is called coal tar creosote, and there is also what is called wood tar creosote. This oil comes from plants that have a distinctive aroma, like creosote. It is a shrub named in the scientific language called Chaparral (Larrea tridentate). So, everything is sometimes also referred to as creosote oil. Creosote oil has many benefits and uses for health; it has been a long time since it was used in the world of traditional medicine. In addition to medicinal purposes, creosote oil is also used significantly in the industry. Oil derived from the creosote Bush, known by the name Chaparral (Larrea Tridentata), is a plant native to the deserts of America and Mexico. It contains a lot of nutrients and medicinal value, which is needed to handle health problems. The essential oil from the creosote plant is obtained from the steam distillation process, as is the marigold oil process.

d. Preparation of Homemade Lotion, Such As Shave Cream & Face Creams, for Dry Skin.

Aim:

To prepare shaving lotion and face creams.

A. Lotion Shave Cream

Ingredients:

- 1/2 cup shea butter
- 1/3 cup sweet almond oil or fractionated coconut oil
- 10 drops of essential oils of choice

Directions:

- Whip shea butter in a bowl
- Slowly add melted coconut or sweet almond oil while whipping.
- Add essential oils and whip.
- Face creams for dry skin

Fig. No 21. – Lotion shave cream

B. Face Creams

Sample Preparation 01:

Ingredients:

- 1 tablespoon peach seed oil.
- 1 tablespoon of almond oil.
- 1 tablespoon of olive oil.
- 1 teaspoon of beeswax.

- Borax powder on the tip of the knife.

- 1 tablespoon hot boiled water

Preparation: Mix the oils and beeswax and put them in a water bath so that the wax melts. Dilute the borax in water. The first formulation is removed from the water bath and immediately mixed with the second composition. Whisk until the cream completely cools.

Fig. No 22. – Face cream

Sample 02:

Ingredients:

- 1 teaspoon of cocoa butter.

- 1 tablespoon of almond oil.

- 1 tablespoon of olive oil.

- 1 teaspoon of beeswax.

- Half a teaspoon of emulsifying wax.

- 2 tablespoons of rose water or mineral water

Preparation: Mix the oils with bees and emulsifying waxes and put them in a water bath. As the mixture melts, remove from the bath and add rose water. Stir or whisk until the cream cools.

Benefits :

1. Sweet Almond Oil

Sweet Almond Oil for the face works like a charm. It is rich in Vitamin E and antioxidants that promote shiny, smooth skin. Regular application can help in reducing scars, blemishes, acne, pigmentation, signs of ageing and sagging skin. Reduction in eye wrinkles, dark circles and eye bags are some of the best known sweet almond oil uses.

2. Peach Oil

Like almonds and apricots, the peach belongs to the family Rosacea. That is why peach kernel oil offers benefits similar to almond oil, apricot oil or plum kernel oil. It is often used as a lipid-replenishing component in shampoos, shower gels and creams. Peach kernel oil has a light texture that absorbs quickly without leaving a sticky film. It protects sensitive, dry and mature skin and can help to strengthen the skin's immune system. Peach kernel oil smooths and hydrates the skin, improves skin elasticity, and leaves a soft and supple feel.

3. Olive Oil

Olive oil acts as an antioxidant, which is a substance that prevents oxidation. Oxidation is a process that can produce free radicals, which are chemicals that can potentially damage cells and may contribute to cancer development. When applied to the skin, antioxidants may prevent premature ageing. Also, some research suggests that putting olive oil on the skin after sun exposure may fight off cancer-causing cells.

4. Rose Water

It Soothes skin irritation and sore throats, reduces skin redness, helps prevent and treat infections, contains antioxidants, heals cuts, scars, and burns, Enhances mood and relieves headaches.

e. Preparation of Dishwasher Powder

Aim:

Preparation of dishwashing powder in a simple way

Ingredients:

Washing Soda, Borax (20 Mule), Bar Soap

Procedure: I – Dish Wash Powder

- Grate the bar soap or mix in the food processor until finely ground. In a large bowl, mix 2 parts washing soda, 2 parts borax and 1 part grated soap. I use 1 bar of grated soap and 1 cup each of washing soda and borax.

- Store in a closed container. I keep mine in quart or half-gallon mason jars. If you are using a big enough container, you can skip step 2 and just put all ingredients in a storage container or jar and shake.

- Use 2 Tablespoons to 1/4 cup per load of laundry

Fig. No 23. – Dish wash powder with blue

Procedure: II – Liquid Laundry Soap.

- Grate one bar of soap with a cheese grater or food processor.

- Put grated soap in a pan with 2 quarts water and gradually heat, stirring constantly until soap is completely dissolved.

- Put 4.5 gallons of really hot tap water in a 5-gallon bucket (available for free in bakeries at grocery stores; just ask them) and stir in 2 cups of borax and 2 cups of Washing Soda until completely dissolved.

- Pour soap mixture from the pan into a 5-gallon bucket. Stir well.

- Cover and leave overnight.

- Shake or stir until smooth and pour into gallon jugs or other containers.

- Use 1/2 to 1 cup per load.

Fig. No 24. – Liquid laundry soap

Benefits: Daily Life – Save Money.

1. Washing Soda

Sodium carbonate (aka washing soda or soda ash) is a highly alkaline substance whose unique chemical composition makes it excellent for household uses, such as degreasing, brightening, and cleaning tough messes.

2. Borax

There are several health benefits of borax, which include the Prevention of Arthritis, swollen throat and tongue sores, relief from painful, swollen red eyes, menstrual problems, cure of urinary infections, enhances testosterone levels, enhancement of female libido, Cure of womb inflammation, and helps in cancer therapy.

f. Laundry Detergents

i) Easy Liquid Laundry Detergent

Ingredients

2/3 cup Super-Washing Soda

3 Tbsp Baking Soda

1/2 cup Liquid Castile soap

5 cups Water

Fig. No 25. – Liquid laundry soap

ii) Easier Liquid Laundry Detergent

2/3 cup Super-Washing Soda

1/2 cup Sal's Suds

4 cups Water

Pour washing soda into a large glass bowl, then slowly stir in 2 cups of boiling water until washing soda is completely dissolved. Stir in Sal's Suds until well combined. Then slowly stir in remaining 2 cups of boiling water. Put it in a glass bottle.

iii) Homemade Fabric Softener

2 cups white vinegar

2 cups distilled water

1/8 cup glycerin

Note:

if you want to have softer clothes, you can simply add a cup of vinegar to your rinse cycle. Don't worry; they won't come out stinking of vinegar! Also, adding baking soda to your load will soften clothes.

Fig. No 26. – Fabric Softener.

Chapter – III

Your Herbal Chemistry

1. Herbal & Excitement in Herbal Life

Many herbs have been used by our ancestors in history. Each and every herb has its own property and usage. Some herbs are very useful in the vapour or liquid form rather than solid (leaves/ stem/ bark/ root) form. There are some herbs that can cure blood vessel cuts and throat infections, germ killers, and bug repellents. It is a god-gifted plant on earth.

2. Experiments

a) Preparation of Homemade Ayurveda Tooth Powder

Aim:

To prepare a homemade sample of ayurvedic tooth powder out of ayurvedic ingredients,

Ingredients required:

1 Tbsp of equal parts neem leaf powder and holy basil powder

1 Tbsp mixture of the powdered herbs of sage, peppermint, clove and cinnamon

1 Tbsp spirulina pinch of rock salt or sea salt

Procedure:

1. Take 1 Tbsp of neem leaf powder and holy basil (Tulsi) leaf powder in a mixing bowl.

2. Make 1 Tbsp of a fine mixture of these herbal powders: sage, peppermint, clove and cinnamon.

3. Add the above-prepared powder to the mixing bowl along with Tulsi and neem powder.

4. Now add about a 1 Tbsp of spirulinar and finely ground sea salt or rock salt into this mixture.

5. Mix all the powders thoroughly and voila! Your Ayurvedic tooth powder is ready.

6. Store this mixture in a clean, airtight container.

Directions for Use

Take a little measure of this tooth powder into your hand. Dip your toothbrush into water and after that, touch the powder with the bristles of your toothbrush and massage your teeth in the usual way, brushing gently.

Benefits:

1. Neem leaf powder

Neem leaf powder purifies the blood, battles free radical damage, flushes out toxins, treats insect bites and cures ulcers. Moreover, the powerful anti-fungal, anti-bacterial properties of neem leaf powder facilitate the treatment of worm infestation, burns, and skin disorders and trigger the immune system.

2. Holy Basil Powder

It has a strong smell and a very intrinsic flavour to it. Citronellol, linalool, cinnamate, geraniol, terpineol and pinene are the various kinds of oil present in basil. There are several benefits of basil powder: it stimulates digestion, helps reduce inflammation, and reduces stress. It also helps to clean our skin from within its essential oils. It helps to remove dirt, pollution and other acne-causing impurities from our skin.

3. Sage

Sage has several proven health benefits. It can help protect the body's cells from damage caused by free radicals due to its high antioxidant capacity, help treat Alzheimer's, Lower blood glucose and cholesterol, and control inflammation.

4. Peppermint

Peppermint, scientifically known as Mentha x Piperitais, is a type of hybrid mint bred through a combination of spearmint and watermint. It has a spicy, refreshing flavour that makes it a popular ingredient in many different foods, candies, and desserts, among others. The leaves of this plant are the primary parts that are used due to the presence of the essential oil, which contains high levels of menthone, menthol, limonene, and various other acids, compounds, and antioxidants. There are a wide range of health effects associated with peppermint, including its ability to relieve hay fever symptoms, prevent nausea and vomiting, and improve memory and cognitive performance, among many others.

5. Clove

It is packed with omega-3 fatty acids and fibre and is rich in minerals (especially magnesium) and vitamins. Minerals found in cloves include iron, magnesium, phosphorus, potassium, sodium, zinc and calcium. The vitamins in clove include thiamin, riboflavin, Vitamin C, niacin, folate, Vitamin B6, Vitamin B12, Vitamin A, Vitamin E, Vitamin K and Vitamin D. To add to the nutritional value, clove possesses various biochemicals such as eugenol, ethanol, thymol, benzene, flavonoids, hexane, and methylene chloride that make it rich in antioxidant, anti-microbial, anti-inflammatory and hepatoprotective properties. It helps in improving digestion by stimulating the secretion of digestive enzymes. It also aids in reducing dyspepsia and nausea. Hepatoprotective properties and antioxidants in clove extracts are helpful in protecting the organs from free radicals. It aids in increasing metabolism and decreases the production of antioxidants in the liver. Extracts of clove are effective against a bacterium that spreads cholera. Moreover, the buds are known to carry strong anti-bacterial properties that are potent enough to kill human pathogens. Bad breath can be cured by consuming the buds of cloves daily. Its bud releases necessary enzymes that kill the bacteria in the mouth that cause bad breath. Clove can be consumed as a power or as a whole bud. Clove oil is known to have healing properties and can be topically applied over rashes, scabies, cuts, wounds, fungal infections, stings, bites and athlete's foot. Make sure the infected area is clean before application.

6. Cinnamon.

Cinnamon is the bark of the tropical trees. It is brown in colour and has a sweet taste that finishes off with a sharp, pungent flavour. This bark is ground to prepare cinnamon powder, which has a coarse texture. The cinnamon powder comes in the form of a sprinkler can or in packet form. Reduces Arthritis Pain, Treats Infertility and Removes Bad Odour. Cinnamon is known for its anti-diabetic properties. It can lower the blood sugar level. It contains some good amounts of antioxidants that will cure the oxidative damage caused to the body by free radicals. This is one of the best health benefits of cinnamon powder. Not only will it recover the damage, but it will also protect the body and fight against any future damage and threats which might be caused by the free radicals in the body. The polyphenols in cinnamon allow this natural powder to perform some unbelievable functions that might not be achieved by any other prescribed medicines. Organic cinnamon powder benefits your skin in many ways! It is loaded with anti-bacterial properties to reduce skin infections like acne, eczema and rashes. Cinnamon has a slightly coarse texture, so it can also exfoliate the skin and remove dead cells.

7. Rock Salt.

Rock salt is loaded with sodium chloride and other different micronutrients such as calcium, magnesium, iron, sulfur, zinc, oxygen, hydrogen, and cobalt. These essentials perform various body functions and keep you healthy and strong. It promotes digestion, boosts metabolism and the immune system, Relieves muscle cramps, treats sore throat, and stabilises blood pressure relief from stress.

Note:

You may change the quantity of herbal composition to suit your taste. To make ayurvedic toothpaste with this tooth powder, add coconut oil to this composition. Remember, there will be no froth while you are brushing.

Fig. No 27. – Ayurvedic Powder

b. Preparation of Ayurvedic Mouthwash Recipe

Aim:

To prepare a homemade sample of an Ayurvedic mouthwash recipe (Triphala Decoction) from Ayurvedic medicines,

Ingredients required:

Triphala powder, one litre (about 4 cups) of water.

Procedure:

Take 40-50 gm (8-10 tsp) of Triphala powder and boil it in one litre (about 4 cups) of water until it is reduced to 250 mL (1 cup). When it cools, filter it with a strainer and keep this preparation in a clean, sterilised bottle.

Use 20-50 ml (2-3 Tbsp) of this decoction as a mouthwash.

You can use it up to 3 times a day. You can also add honey and rock salt or sea salt according to your palatability. This will enhance its effectiveness.

Fig. No 28. – Ayurvedic Mouthwash

Benefits of Triphala Decoction:

This homemade mouthwash recipe is easy to make and inexpensive. It is free of any chemicals and alcohol which has harmful effects on the oral cavity. This mouthwash is 100% safe, natural, inexpensive and has no side effects. It can also be used safely by children.

Triphala has anti-caries activity. It is valuable in the prevention and treatment of several diseases of the mouth such as dental caries, spongy, bleeding gums, gingivitis, and stomatitis. It prevents the accumulation of acids and plaque formation on the surface of the tooth, and thus prevents further demineralisation and the breakdown of tooth enamel. It has the same action on bacteria as that of Chlorhexidine mouthwash usually recommended by dentists for treating plaque.

One study showed that Triphala mouthwash with oral powder of Triphala used over a period of one month reduced tooth mobility, pocket depth, bleeding gums, sensitivity to heat and cold, and calculus formation with minimal recurrence in all the clinical parameters.[14]

Result

A homemade sample of the ayurvedic mouthwash recipe (**Triphala Decoction**) is prepared.

C. Traditional Method of Making Amla Oil

Aim:

Prepare a homemade sample of amla oil and calculate the fatty acid present in it.

Ingredients Required:

This is a traditional ayurvedic approach to making amla oil. It's slightly tricky and time-consuming and takes about 2 to 3 hours to prepare. 120-gram amla powder, 250ml coconut oil or sesame oil, olive or sunflower or avocado oil, 1 litre water.

Procedure:

Combine 100 grams of amla powder with 1 litre of water in a pan. Bring to a boil, reduce the flame, and simmer until approximately half of the liquid has evaporated. Then strain this amla concentrate. Next, take a thick bottom stainless-steel pan, place the coconut oil, remaining amla powder (20 grams), and the amla concentrate that you made (approx. 500 ml). Bring to a boil, then reduce the flame and let this mixture simmer very slowly until all the water has evaporated. When it's done, the oil will appear yellow and transparent, and you will be able to see the dark bottom, which is caused by amla ash. Once done, strain immediately and store in a glass jar or bottle away from direct sunlight.

Fig. No 29. – Amla Oil

Adding Other Herbs:

Along with amla you can also add various hair beneficial herbs such as brahmi for strengthening, bhringraj for greying, methi (fenugreek) and hibiscus for conditioning, rosemary and sage for hair loss, lavender and chamomile for scalp conditions, and calendula for shine.

Note:

When adding any herb, keep the oil-to-herb ratio roughly the same. So you will have to reduce the quantity of amla powder and add herbs of your choice or increase the oil content.

Benefits:

Hair will feel healthy and soft, with added shine and volume. Reduce hair loss.

d. Preparation of Natural Insect Repellent Spray

Aim:

Prepare sample headache bam using peppermint, oil and wax

Ingredients Required:

- 03 tbsp shea butter,
- 03 tbsp beeswax,
- 03 tbsp coconut oil,
- 20 drops of peppermint, essential oil
- 15 drops of lavender essential oil,
- 15 drops of tea tree essential oil,
- 05 drops of eucalyptus essential oil.

Procedure:

Fig. No 30. –Mosquito repellent Oil (Photos 1 to 4)

- Get the containers ready and set aside.

- Measure the shea butter, beeswax, and coconut oils. (photo 1)

- Put the oils in a microwavable glass bowl. Heat for just 45 seconds to 1 minute until completely melted (photo 2)

- Allow the mix to cool for a few minutes. When the bowl is no longer hot to the touch, add the essential oils. (photo 3)

- Pour the mix into your containers and let cool.

- You can also place them in the refrigerator for a few minutes to harden the mix.

- Simply rub a tiny amount into the temples, onto your forehead, or the back of your neck to instantly soothe your headache.

Fig. No 31. —Mosquito repellent spray

Benefits:

1. Shea Butter

Shea butter contains vitamins A and E, which are well-known for their beneficial properties that promote healthy skin and reduce the signs of ageing. It is also a rich source of fatty acids, which are essential for nourishing the skin and reducing inflammation.

2. Beeswax

Beeswax has non-allergenic properties that can make it useful in protecting the skin from airborne allergens. It also provides slight anti-inflammatory and antioxidant qualities, which can benefit the body.

3. Coconut oil

Coconut oil has many nutrients that can contribute to your health and to a good diet. It's full of fatty acids that your body needs and may help improve cognitive function, metabolism, and hair and skin health.

4. Lavender Oil

Lavender oil is a beneficial nectar extracted from the distinctive purple flowers of the lavender plant. This aromatic shrub, commonly known as English lavender (*Lavandula angustifolia*), originated in the western Mediterranean region and is now cultivated throughout the U.S., Europe, and Australia. A major reason for its popularity is that the oil from this plant boasts many health-supporting properties.

5. Tea Tree

Active ingredients like terpene hydrocarbons, monoterpenes, and sesquiterpenes are found abundantly in tea trees, and these compounds enhance the tea tree's anti-bacterial, antiviral, and anti-fungal activity. Tea tree oil or cream can be applied to skin infections such as athlete's foot and ringworm, as well as to corns, warts, acne and boils, infected burns, scrapes, wounds, insect bites and stings, and other skin conditions. The herb is effective in mouthwashes, countering oral infection and gum disease, and it can also be used as a gargle for sore throats. Due to its anti-bacterial, anti-microbial and antiseptic compounds, Tea Tree essential oil is an effective wound healer that prevents infection. The anti-microbial and anti-inflammatory properties of Tea Tree make it a widespread essential oil for the treatment of acne, calming redness, swelling and inflammation. Tea Trees may also reduce the appearance of acne scars. Tea tree, and its essential oil, is one of the most important natural antiseptics, and it merits a place in every medicine chest. It is useful for treating stings, burns, wounds and skin infections of all kinds. An essential oil obtained from the leaves and twigs is strongly antiseptic, diaphoretic and expectorant. It encourages the immune system and is effective against a broad range of bacterial and fungal infections. It is used in the treatment of chronic and some acute infections, notably cystitis, glandular fever and chronic fatigue syndrome. It is used externally in the treatment of thrush, vaginal infections, acne, athlete's foot, verrucae, warts, insect bites, cold sores and nits. It is applied neatly to verrucae, warts, and nits but is diluted with carrier oil, such as almond oil, for other uses. Indigenous Australians of eastern inland areas use "tea trees" as a traditional medicine by inhaling the oils from the crushed leaves to treat coughs and colds. They also sprinkle leaves on wounds, after which a poultice is applied. Tea tree leaves are soaked to make an infusion to treat sore throats or skin ailments. It is also known to reduce inflammation and may be effective in the treatment of fungal infections such as athlete's foot. Oil has been proven to treat topical bacterial (acne), fungal (athlete's foot), and viral infections in humans. It has been effective in curing respiratory problems such as bronchitis and asthma. When converted into mouthwash or toothpaste, it can kill canker sores, bad breath, and gum disease. It is used as an antiseptic and disinfectant for wounds and heals burns. It is also effective for the treatment of dandruff and scalp problems. It can be used for treatment of bleeding gums, gingivitis and periodontal disease. It is useful for treating stings, burns, wounds and skin infections of all kinds. It stimulates the immune system and is effective against a broad range of bacterial and fungal infections. It is used in the treatment of chronic and some acute infections, notably cystitis, glandular fever and chronic fatigue syndrome. It is used externally in the treatment of thrush, vaginal infections, acne, athlete's foot, verrucae, warts, insect bites, cold sores and nits. It is an active ingredient in many topical preparations for the treatment of cutaneous infections, including wound infections, fungal dermatoses, otitis media, and acne.

6. Eucalyptus essential oil

Eucalyptus oil has been discovered to possess anti-bacterial, anti-fungal, and antiviral actions. Cineole, the key compound present in eucalyptus essential oil, is renowned for its anti-bacterial properties. Thus, it is helpful in cleansing the epidermis and ridding the pores of harmful toxins and impurities that contribute to a variety of skin conditions. The result is a complexion that is deeply purified and healthier than ever. Its anti-inflammatory and pain-relieving properties, coupled with its normal cooling feeling, create eucalyptus oil perfect for soothing a painful sunburn. Anti-bacterial properties also shield skin from illness.

Chapter IV

Your Aroma Chemistry

Aroma Chemistry deals with essential oils and volatile oils. Essential oils constituents can be divided into 2 major groups: terpene hydrocarbons and oxygenated compounds. Based on the hydrocarbons and oxygenated compounds, the odour may be varied. These different codes are used in order to express its fragrance. Essential oil's shelf life is dependent on the following 3 factors.

a) Oxygen,   b) Heat,   c) Light.

In general, shelf life is determined by the chemical composition of the essential oils, some of which oxidise or evaporate faster than others. Essential Oils, which have a lot of monoterpenes or oxides, have the shortest shelf life, which is around about 1 -2 years. Essential Oils, which contain a lot of phenols, may last up to 3 years. The essential oils that contain ketones, monoterpenols, and/ or esters usually have a shelf life of 4-5 years. The essential oils that contain lots of sesquiterpenes and sesquiterpenols can last up to 6 years.

I. Some Essentials and their Details

1. Common Essential Oils Shelf Life

1 year: Citrus fruit, Neroli, lemongrass, frankincense, tea tree, pine and spruce oils

2 -3 years: Virtually every other essential oil

4 -8 years: Sandalwood, Vetiver, patchouli

2. Shelf Life of Common Carrier Oils

Almond Oil (refined, expeller pressed)	–	1 year
Aloe Vera Oil	–	6 months – 1 year
Apricot Kernel Oil (cold pressed)	–	1 year
Argan Oil (cold pressed/unrefined)	–	2+ years
Avocado Oil (cold pressed/ unrefined)	–	1 year
Borage Oil	–	6 months (may go rancid more quickly if not refrigerated)
Brazil Nut Oil	–	2 years
Calendula Oil (infused)	–	1 year
Camellia Oil	–	2 years

Carrot Seed Oil (cold pressed)	–	1 year
Castor Oil (cold pressed)	–	5 years
Chia Seed Oil (cold pressed)	–	2 years
Coconut Oil (cold pressed/ unrefined)	–	2-4 years
Cranberry Seed Oil	–	2 years
Emu Oil	–	1 year (refrigerated)
Evening Primrose Oil (cold pressed)	–	6 months – 1 year
Flax Seed Oil	–	6 months (refrigerated)
Fractionated Coconut Oil	–	5+ years
Grapeseed Oil (cold pressed)	–	1 year
Hazelnut Oil (cold pressed)	–	1 year
Hemp Seed Oil (cold pressed)	–	1 year (refrigerated)
Hypericum Oil (St John's Wort – infused)	–	1 year
Jojoba Oil (cold pressed)	–	5 years
Macadamia Nut Oil (cold pressed)	–	1 year

Moringa Seed Oil	–	1+ years
Neem Oil (cold pressed/ unrefined)	–	2 years
Olive Oil (cold pressed/unrefined)	–	2 years
Palm Oil (Red – unrefined)	–	2 years
Papaya Seed Oil (cold pressed)	–	1 year
Passion Fruit Seed Oil (Maracuja Oil – cold pressed)	–	1-2 years
Peach Kernel Oil (cold pressed/ unrefined)	–	1 year
Pecan Nut Oil (cold pressed/ unrefined)	–	1 year
Pomegranate Seed Oil	–	1 year
Poppy Seed Oil	–	1 year
Rose Hip Seed Oil	–	6 months (refrigerated)
Safflower Seed Oil (high linoleic)	–	2 years
Safflower Seed Oil (high oleic)	–	2 years
Sesame Oil (cold pressed)	–	1 year
Shea Oil	–	1 year
Soybean Oil (refined)	–	1 year

Sunflower Seed Oil (cold pressed/ unrefined)	–	1 year
Tamanu Oil (cold pressed/ unrefined)	–	1 year
Walnut Oil (unrefined)	–	2 years
Wheat Germ Oil (unrefined)	–	1 year

2. Blending Process

Blending Process is the process of mixing carrier oil with suitable essential oils. There are 3 notes used: base note, middle note and top note. Mostly base notes are used to select the carrier oils. Here are some of the important notes.

i. Blending details

Top Notes	Middle Notes	Base Notes
Anise	Bay	Angelica
Basil	Cajuput	Cedarwood
Bergamot	Camphor	Cinnamon
Boronia	Cardamom	Clove
Citronella	Carrot seed	Frankincense
Fennel	Chamomile, German	Ginger

Top Notes	Middle Notes	Base Notes
Eucalyptus	Chamomile, Roman	Helichrysum
Grapefruit	Clary sage	Jasmine
Lemon	Clove	Myrrh
Lemongrass	Cypress	Neroli
Lime	Dill	Patchouli
Mandarin	Eucalyptus Radiata	Pepper, black
Myrtle, Lemon	Fennel	Rose
Orange, sweet	Geranium	Sandalwood
Orange, bitter	Geranium rose	Vetiver
Peppermint	Ginger	Ylang ylang

ii. Dilution Table

The number of essential oil drops and their percentages

Dilution %	10ml (Base Oil)	15ml	20ml	30ml (1 oz)	60 ml (2 oz)
0.50%	1 E.O drop	2	3	4	8
1%	3	4	6	9	18
2%	6	9	12	18	36

Dilution %	10ml (Base Oil)	15ml	20ml	30ml (1 oz)	60 ml (2 oz)
3%	9	13	18	27	54
4%	12	18	24	36	72
5%	15	22	30	45	90

2 Tbsp = 1 fl.oz = 30 ml = 6 tsp

1 tsp = 5 ml = 100 drops.

1 tsp of carrier oil and add one drop of EO = 1%

iii. Essential Oil Conversions

Ounces	Millilitres
1/8th oz	3.75 mls
1/4th oz	7.5 mls
1/2 oz	15 mls
1 oz	30 mls
4 oz	120 mls
8 oz	237 mls
16 oz	473 mls

iv. Diluting by Age Group

A. *2 – 6 years – 0.25% Dilution (1 drop per 4 teaspoons of carrier oil)*

Hydrosols and herbs are still a good choice for this age group and should be considered before essential oils.

B. *Over 6 years of age – 1% dilution (1 drop per teaspoon of carrier oil; 6 drops per ounce)*

Recommended for children over age 6, pregnant women, elderly adults, and those who have sensitive skin, compromised immune systems, or other serious health issues.

C. *Average healthy adult – 2% dilution (2 drops per teaspoon of carrier oil; 12 drops per ounce)*

Ideal for most adults and in most situations.

D. *Temporary health issue – 3% – 10% dilution (2-20 drops per teaspoon of carrier oil; 12-120 drops per ounce)*

Best used short-term for a temporary health issue, such as a muscle injury or respiratory congestion. For an acute issue, such as a muscle cramp or severe pain, 25% may be appropriate

(25 drops per teaspoon of carrier oil; 150 drops per ounce)

3. Experiments

The following mixers or blends may be used in the rollers or vials or in the form of balm, gel or liquids in the kitchen chemistry.

A. Body Scrubs

It's time to make some body scrubs

There are 3 main types of scrubs

i) Chamomile Oatmeal scrub

50 gms Cornmeal

35 gms rolled oats

35 gms finely ground almonds

2 Tbs Jojoba oil

8 drops chamomile EO

6 drops Geranium

Procedure

Grind oats, cornmeal, and almonds in a coffee grinder to create a fine texture. Put them in a glass container with the EO's. When you are ready to use it, add the jojoba oil to the mixture.

ii) Brown Sugar Body Scrub

1/2 cup brown sugar

4 Tbs jojoba oil

2 Tbs Glycerine (optional)

6 drops sandalwood EO

10 drops Lavender EO

Mix and use.

iii) Honey and Yoghurt Scrub

1⁄4 cup finely ground rolled oats

1⁄4 cup wheat bran

2 Tbs jojoba oil

2 Tbsp Raw Honey

1⁄2 cup natural yoghurt

10 drops lavender EO

4 drops Rose EO

4 drops Chamomile EO

Mix oats, wheat bran, and EOs. You can then store these until you are ready to use them. When you want to use them, you add the other ingredients. (This is great for people with sensitive skin)

iv) Lemon Sugar Scrub

250 gms sugar

100mls jojoba oil

20 drops lemon EO

Combine and use.

v) Minty Salt Scrub

500 gms sea salt

200 mls favourite carrier oil(look at carrier oil section to see qualities of each)

10 drops peppermint EO

10 drops Spearmint EO

9 drops Lemon EO

Combine and use

Fig. No 32. – Essential Oil in the colour bottle – Overview picture

Fig. No 33. – Cross-section photo of the Essential Oil

b. Foot Scrub Recipe

Nothing feels better than a foot scrub when you have made your own scrub!

i) Easy Foot Scrub Recipe

1 cup of sea salt(or Epsom salts or granulated sugar)

1 Tbsp coconut oil (you can use any carrier oils)

1 Tbsp Olive oil

20 drops of essential oil (peppermint, tea tree, and lavender is a great combination

5 drops of each, or just use one EO)

You could also add baking soda as well

Mix and keep in an airtight jar

Fig. No 34. –Base Foot Scrub Recipe

c. Balms

Here are some great recipes to try with your balm base that you have made!

i) Cold and Flu Chest Rub Balm

In 20 mls of natural balm base mix:

8 drops of Eucalyptus

6 drops of Black Pepper

4 drops of Peppermint

4 drops of Rosemary

Apply to the chest day and night to ease the symptoms of coughs and colds.

ii) Coconut & sweet orange lip balm

In 20 mls of natural balm base mix:

5 drops of Sweet Orange (or any other favourite EO) - do not use bergamot or lime; they are phototoxic, in other words, if you go out into the sun, your lips can burn)

Apply a small amount to lips when needed to smooth and soften. Do not apply to cracked or broken skin.

iii) Headache Balm

In 20 mls of natural balm base mix:

6 drops of Lavender

8 drops of Rosemary

4 drops of Peppermint

3 drops of Eucalyptus

Apply to temples and forehead

iv) Eczema Skin Relief Balm

1/4 cup shea butter

3 tablespoons beeswax pastilles

3 tablespoons almond oil

1/4 cup raw honey

25 drops of lavender essential oil

20 drops of Sandalwood essential oil

15 drops German or Roman Chamomile

Place the coconut oil, shea butter and beeswax in a double boiler or microwave. Remove the jar from the water and set aside for 5 minutes to cool slightly. Add the honey and essential oils and stir to combine. Transfer the balm to a small tin or lidded glass jar and let it cool completely.

Fig. No 35. –Headache Balm.

d. Bath Bombs

i) Bath Bomb Ingredients

8 ounces baking soda (about 1 cup)

4 ounces citric acid (1/2 cup)

1/2 cup (4 ounces) sea salt or Epsom salt

4 ounces cornstarch (about 3/4 cup)

3 TBSP carrier oil of choice

2 tsp witch hazel (or water) plus a little more, if needed, 30-40 drops of essential oils

Instructions

Combine dry ingredients (baking soda, salt, citric acid, and cornstarch) in a large bowl and mix well until combined. Add the liquid ingredients to the dry ingredients, a few drops at a time. Mix well with your hands (wear gloves if you have sensitive skin). The mixture should hold together when squeezed without crumbling. It may need to add slightly more witch hazel if it hasn't achieved this consistency yet. It is recommended to use a spray bottle with additional liquid to add evenly. Quickly push the mixture into moulds, greased muffin tins or ice cube trays. Press in firmly and leave for at least 24 hours (48 is better) or until hardened. It will expand some, and this is normal. Then, it is pushed down into the mould several times while it is drying to keep it from expanding too much. Using the metal moulds will create a stronger and more effective final bath bomb. When dry, remove and store in an airtight container or bag.

ii) Toilet Bowl Bombs

Toilet bowl fizzy tablets

2 cups baking soda

1/2 cup citric acid

30 drops of essential oil

Water or hydrogen peroxide to spray on. Add baking soda and citric acid, stir, add essential oils, and combine. Spray the water onto the correct consistency (wet sand), then put it into trays. Wait for a few hours or overnight for them to harden. Remove and put in an airtight container.

iii) Bath Salts Formula

Here is a simple bath salts formula that you can expand upon if you want.

This is great; all you need to do is add the essential oils that you desire and

put a tablespoon or so of the bath salts into your bath. You can store them

in a mason jar.

1 cup of Epsom salts

1/4 cup sea salt

1/4 cup baking soda

3 Tbsp Carrier oil of your choice

25 Essential oils total

Combine the carrier oil with the essential oils and mix them, then add them to your dry ingredients.

Put in about 1/4 to a 1/2 cup for your bath.

Fig. No 36. – Bath Bomb

e. Ideas for Aromatherapy Inhalers

Calming Blend

25 drops Lavender

15 drops of Chamomile

i) Allergy Relief 1

15 drops Eucalyptus radiata

15 drops Rosemary ct. cineole (Rosmarinus officinalis ct. cineole)

10 drops Bay Laurel (Laurus nobilis)

ii) Allergy Relief 2

12 drops Lemon (Citrus limon)

12 drops Rosemary ct. cineole (Rosmarinus officinalis ct. cineole)

12 drops Tea tree (Melaleuca alternifolia)

iii) Colds and Flus

10 drops Scotch Pine (Pinus sylvestris)

12 drops Douglas Fir (Pseudotsuga menzies)

12 drops Eucalyptus radiate

Fig. No 37. – Inhaler

f. Roller Bottle Blends

i) Headache Relief

5 drops peppermint

5 drops lavender

3 drops chamomile

ii) Stress Relief

5 drops peppermint

3 drops frankincense

3 drops lavender

3 drops chamomile

iii) Colds and Flus

5 drops peppermint

3 drops eucalyptus

3 drops lemon

3 drops rosemary

iv) Anxiety Relief

6 drops bergamot

6 drops frankincense

v) Relax

5 drops lavender

4 drops clary sage

3 drops ylang ylang

2 drops marjoram

vi) Immune Booster

3 drops oregano

3 drops melaleuca

3 drops lemon

3 drops frankincense

3 drops cinnamon

vii) Stomach Problems

4 drops ginger

3 drops peppermint

3 drops fennel

2 drops coriander

2 drops lemon

viii) Muscular Relief

4 wintergreen

4 peppermint

3 juniper

3 lemongrass

ix) Bug Bite Relief (For Itching)

4 drops lavender

4 drops peppermint

3 drops frankincense

3 drops melaleuca

3 drops lemon

x) Chillout

6 drops vetiver

6 drops cedarwood

xi) Sleep Aid

6 drops lavender

6 drops clary sage

xii) Energy Booster

4 drops of wild orange

4 drops frankincense

4 drops cinnamon

xiii) Focus and Concentration

6 drops of wild orange

6 drops peppermint

xiv) Positivity

4 drops grapefruit

4 drops of wild orange

3 drops lemon

2 drops bergamot

xv) Acne Helper

5 drops melaleuca

5 drops lavender

3 drops lemongrass

Fig. No 38. – Overview Roller bottle

g. Lavender Bath Salts

Bath salts are wonderful! This is so easy to do and makes a great gift!

Ingredients

4 cups of Epsom salts

2 cup baking soda

40 drops Lavender EO

Combine and use.

Fig. No 39. – Lavender bath salts

h. Muscle Balms, Tiger Balm and Slave

i) Instant Muscle Relief Balm

1/2 cup Coconut Oil

1/4 cup Grated Beeswax

2 tsp Cayenne Powder

3 tsp Turmeric Powder

10 drops Peppermint EO

10 drops Lavender EO

1 Glass Jar

Gently melt the beeswax and coconut oil, add the cayenne pepper and turmeric. Let it cool slightly, and add the EOs. Mix through and put it in a jar.

ii) Herbal Pain Salve

1/2 ounce Beeswax

2 ounces of Coconut Oil

15 drops Eucalyptus EO

15 drops Peppermint EO

7 drops Clove EO

1 Glass Jar

Gently melt the beeswax and coconut oil in the double boiler, let it cool slightly and add the EOs. Put it in a jar.

iii) Homemade Tiger Balm

Double boiler

1/4 cup olive oil

10 oz beeswax

12 drops Camphor EO

12 drops Peppermint EO

10 drops Eucalyptus EO

7 drops Cinnamon EO

7 drops Clove EO

Gently melt the beeswax and coconut oil in the double boiler, let it cool slightly and add the EOs. Put it in a jar.

iv) Sprain Care Oil

Use this for acute sprains. It works great!

3 Tbsp Avocado Oil

3 Tbsp Castor Oil

2 Tbsp Hemp Seed Oil

2 tsp Turmeric Powder

7 drops Peppermint EO

7 drops Lavender EO

7 drops Wintergreen EO

2 Airtight Glass Jar

Combine and use

v) Peppermint Window and Mirror Cleaner

No need for windex ever again!

Ingredients:

¼ cupping rubbing alcohol

¼ cup white vinegar

4 cups filtered water

30 drops peppermint EO

1 spray bottle

Mix all ingredients together in a spray bottle and shake, and that is it!

i. Room Sprays

Here are lots of ideas that you can use for your room sprays. Use about 40 drops of essential oils in a 16 oz (500mls) spray bottle. You can always use more or less depending on the strength that you like. Remember to add 25% of a grain alcohol such as ever clear to your distilled water that will stop microbial growth.

i) Herbs Delight

30 drops lemon

9 drops rosemary

7 drops thyme

7 drops spearmint

ii) Clean Forest

12 drops pine

10 drops cedarwood

12 drops lavender

10 drops spearmint

iii) Inner Beauty

10 drops cedarwood

12 drops orange

12 drops lavender

7 drops spearmint

7 drops frankincense

iv) Sunday Afternoon

25 drops lavender

25 drops lime

10 drops spearmint

v) Insect Blend

12 drops peppermint

12 drops lemongrass

12 drops lemon eucalyptus

vi) By the Fireplace

22 drops wintergreen

12 drops lemongrass

12 drops juniper berry

vii) Happy Days

10 drops lime

12 drops grapefruit

12 drops tangerine

12 drops spearmint

viii) Refreshing

15 drops spearmint

17 drops tangerine

12 drops bergamot

ix) Citrus Mint

22 drops lemon

05 drops basil

07 drops spearmint

x) Warming Spices

17 drops orange

12 drops ginger

12 drops ylang ylang

xi) Wintery Nights

17 drops lavender

17 drops cedarwood

12 drops spruce

xii) Citrus Sensation

12 drops grapefruit

12 drops orange

05 drops lemon

07 drops bergamot

xiii) Energy Booster

17 drops bergamot

17 drops lemon

12 drops cypress

xiv) Romance

12 drops ylang ylang

12 drops orange

12 drops sandalwood

05 drops patchouli

xv) Smile Time

17 drops tangerine

12 drops lavender

05 drops lime

05 drops spearmint

Fig. No 40. – Room Sprayer

j. Wood Furniture Polish

i) Wood Furniture Polish I

1 Tbsp Olive Oil

1/4 cup White Vinegar

12 drops Lemon EO

12 drops Cedarwood EO

07 drops Orange EO

A 4 ounce Spray Bottle

Mix together and shake before use

ii) Wood Furniture Polish II

1 1/2 cups Olive Oil

1/2 cup Beeswax

12 drops Lemon EO

10 drops Cedarwood EO

7 drops Orange EO

1 Mason Jar

Melt in the double boiler the beeswax, combine the other oils.

Fig. No 41. – Wood Furniture polish

Chapter V

Glass chemistry in Kitchen

1. Etching & Staining Science

Glass is an Inorganic solid compound. It can be translucent or transparent. The glasses differ in colour, thickness, and property based on the chemical composition present in them. The main constituent of glass is silicon dioxide. The solid-state of glass is achieved by cooling the molten state of glass materials so that the internal arrangement of atoms or molecules is arranged systematically or randomly.

Glass Etching:

Etching is a technique which helps to remove the surface of the glass. It is the process of treating areas of glass surface to create a coarsened or scratched or roughened, frosted glass design. In this technique many varieties of creams are used such as armour etch cream, Glassica cream, Etchall, Fixyetch etc., Hydrogen Fluoride is one of the chemicals in all the above etching cream. HF reacts with glass (SiO_2).

$$SiO_2 + 4HF \rightarrow SiF_4 + 2H_2O$$

SiF4 is not a solid that consists of vertex-connected tetrahedra like SiO_2 but is a gas at room temperature. Technically, HF is not a solvent since in this case it reacts with the glass vessel.

Fig. No 42. – Etched Glass

Glass Staining:

Colouring or creating patterns on the glass surface by using solvent oil-based paints is called staining or glass staining. It is a liquid-leading process. Glass stains can be applied to anything glass: ornaments, sun catchers, glass bottles, windows, dishes, vases…It is the oldest technique in history, which provides a better appearance and is resistant to glass. Some products are available in the market that give fine colours to the glass, such as fevicryl (opaque), Vitrea 160 (transparent), Hobby Ideas (opaque), etc.

Fig. No 43. –Stained Glass

2. Experiments

a) Glass Etching & Staining Science

Aim:

Etch and engrave a glass jar using an etching paste and an engraving pen.

Materials:

Glassica Etching paste, Engrave single point Pen, Glass jar, 3A Battery, Stencil Sheets, Notepad and stationary items.

Procedure:

i) Etching Process:

Create your pattern using masking or black tape. Wash the glass jar well in warm, soapy water and place it in the oven (in a controlled way) for some time or in sunlight. Apply your black or masking tape design onto the glass jar. Be sure to have a smooth surface on the glass surface before pasting it. Use a single popsicle stick to seal down every single edge of black or masking tape. Use a light or sponge brush to apply a thick layer of etching cream to the exposed glass portions of your glass jar. Let etching cream sit for 10 to 15 minutes.

Rinse the cream thoroughly with warm water, followed by cold water. Remove tape. Your etched design will be visible once the glass is completely dry!

ii) Glass Staining:

Liquid Leading Process

Sketch the design onto a glass/ceramic bowl. Wash the bowl well in warm - soapy water. Rinse with warm water. Dry completely. Hold the Liquid Leading bottle 0.5- inch above the surface of your glass / ceramic bowl, and squeeze to create your design. Let it dry for 12 hours. To stain glass, dip brush desired colour and drip stain onto segments of glass/ ceramic bowl. Mildly feast stain until it covers the entire area. Leave your glass bowl to dry for a few days to seal your design.

Result:

Glass Etching and staining process discussed.

Chapter – VI

Glass Chemistry in Lab

Glass Cutting, Glass Bending, Glass Fusion & Glass Blowing - Endeavour Science

a. Glass Science –Bending Methods

Aim

Bend a Borosilicate and Soda-Glass glass/ tube using Bunsen burner and to know the basic techniques of bending glass tubes using a simple process.

Materials Needed

Measuring tape. 30-35 cm long Soda-Glass tube.

Procedure:

The Process of Bending the Glass Tube.

Materials Required:

- 30-35 cm long Soda-glass tube
- Bunsen Burner

Procedure:

Hold the tube with both hands slightly horizontally, in flame from the oxygen LPG mixer burner. Score or mark the point of bending of the glass with fine-tuned flame. Keep rotating the soda tube with the help of thumbs and fingers while heating so that the tube is heated and softened uniformly. Slowly bend the glass without wasting the flame and molten part. On rotation, the molten glass gets uniformly bounded up in the scoring point. Continuously keep the glass tube in the flame till it becomes bent. Apply gentle pressure on the glass tube where it is softened, and bend the glass tube at the desired angle. Remove from the flame when the desired angle is formed, and the glass tube is bent. Cool it by placing it on a ceramic plate.

Protections to Be Taken During the Experiment:

- 5-7 cm length of the tube for the bending process.

- Wear glasses and stand at a suitable distance.

- Never give or overpressure on the glass tube when it is in a hot state.

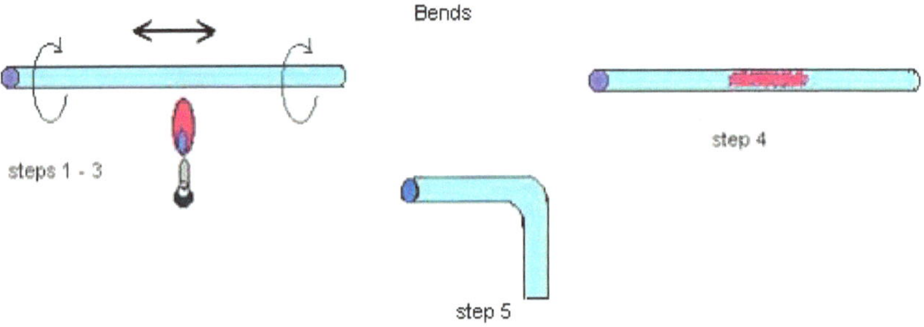

Fig. No 44. – View of Glass bending.

Result:

A borosilicate glass tube/ Soda-Glass tube is bent at different angles.

b. Glass Science – Cutting methods

Aim:

Cut a Borosilicate and Soda-Glass glass/ tube using circular glass cutters / Triangular Files / Machines.

Materials Needed:

Glass Tubes, Glass Plates, Glass Cutters, triangular files, Wet cloth, Cutting Machine. Measuring tape.

Procedure:

I. Cutting method using a triangular file

Mark the area to be cut with a triangular file on the glass tube. Place your fingers on the glass, tune on the opposite side, and quickly scratch downward. Eliminate the sharp edges of the tube with suitable power.

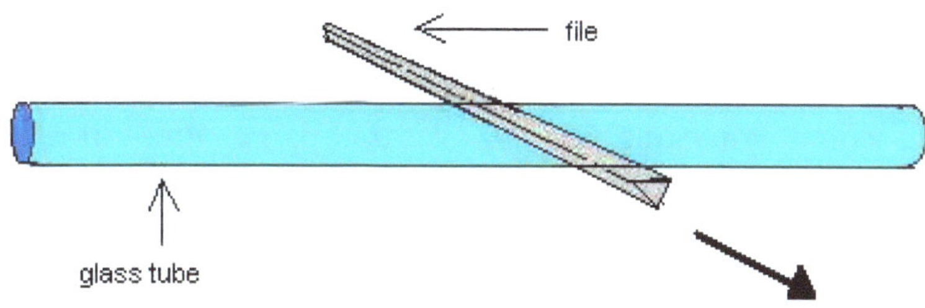

Fig. No 45. – Glass cutting view

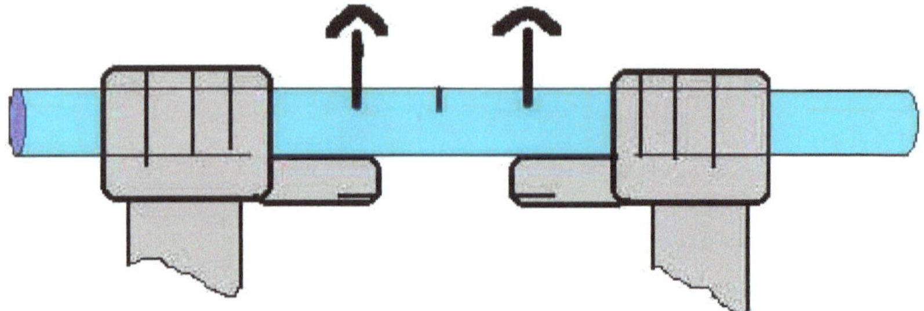

Fig. No 46. – Scoring and hand pressure method

II. The cutting method uses circular glass cutters.

1. Make a score/ cut on the flat glass plates using a circular cutter blade. Make sure before scoring that there are no marks on the glass flat surface. Use a scale or measuring tape to mark the length of the portions on the surface in which to be cut…

2. Make a one sharp and one time score on the surface by giving hand pressure on the glass cutting tool or Put the cutter on the glass plate and try to get a feel of how much pressure to use, as you cut, try to keep about the same pressure and speed the whole way.

3. Keep the cutter at a straight angle right/left and slightly tilted toward you.

4. Cut/score only once! If, by any chance, parts of the line were not scored, you can try to run over that part again., but ideally, you should only need to do it all in one move.

5. There are 3 ways of doing or separating the scoring part.

    a. "The Shocker," hitting the glass on the opposite side of the score from one end to the other of the glass. (Note: The disadvantage with this method is that every time you beat the glass, you risk that the cut will start travelling to the left or right away from the score, especially if you're not good at hitting right under the score)

b. "The casual" - Only with the help of your hands, break open the score. Place your 2 pointer fingers on the underside of the glass, one on each side of the score. Put your 2 thumbs on the top of the glass, one on each side of the score, and just break it open like you would break a chocolate bar. The danger with this is that your hands surround the edge of the glass and are more exposed to cuts if you're not careful or have a little mishap. (Caution: Do not try this on any glass thicker than 5 mm if you don't have some experience with this method)

c. The safest and most controllable way of breaking the glass on most thicknesses of glass is using plastic /wood glass cutters. The cutter can be any wooden or plastic piece 3-5mm / 1/8 inch thick, and 1 cm / 1/2 inch wide. Then place one palm on each side of the cutter, resting them flat and firm on the glass. Give the glass a good push straight down towards the surface.

Fig. No 47.. – Modern portable Glass Cutter

III. Machine Cutting

1. If the thickness is more or a large cylindrical tube, it should be cut with a glass lathe.

2. Place the large cylindrical tube in the fixture which is given in the glass lathe.

3. Adjust the pressure screws to hold the large tube in a stationary way.

4. Rotate the tube clockwise with a power-connected circulatory hand in the glass lathe.

5. Enable the circular blade grinder to touch the cylindrical tube. Please note a soft touch is enough to create a score on the glass surface.

6. Pour lubricant or water drops on the score to reduce the heat on the surface.

7. Use a holding pressure gauge to create a pressure on the scoring place and thus the tube is separated.

8. Cut tubes may be collected in a safe place for further laboratory use.

Fig. No 48.. – Automatic class cutter machine

Result:

A borosilicate glass tube/ Soda-Glass tube is cut via a triangle file and glass cutters.

c. Glass Science –Blowing Methods

Blowing a Bulb in a Tube.

There are many methods in the scientific glass world for blowing a bulb. Here, we discussed a common method which is suitable for any type of chemistry lab-provided compressed motor and Oxy-LPG cylinders.

The glass tube is selected with one end closed, but it should be cut a little longer, say about 12 inches. Beginning at a point about 4 inches from the closed end, glass is collected and blown into a thick-walled bulb. Greater care must be taken, however, that the cylinder collected and this thick bulb are of uniform thickness and set squarely in the axis of the tube. Instead of removing the tail, the bulb must be blown in this case with both pieces of tubing attached, and care must be taken that they "line up" properly, i.e., are in the same straight line and that this line passes as near as may be through the centre of the bulb. The tube is held in an approximately horizontal position during the blowing of the bulb, as in the previous case, and special care is taken with the rotation. Both pieces of the tube must, of course, be rotated at the same rate, and their softened ends must be kept at exactly the proper distance from each other so that the bulb may be spherical and not elongated. If the blowing of the bulb is quickly and accurately done, it may usually be completed before the glass is quite set, and the alignment of the 2 tubes may then be rectified while looking straight through the bore of the tube.

Points to Remember (in Short)

How to Blow a Bulb?

Take a good piece of glass tube about 3/4 inch in diameter and 15 inches long; draw one end out long and thin for about 3 inches as shown at A in below Figure 49. Then heat a small part of the tube in a large or brush flame, turn the glass in the flame all the time until it is soft and then press on both ends to make the glass thicker at this point. Do the same thing above the ring thus formed, and so on, until you have several rings of glass, as shown at B, which are thick enough to make the sized bulb you want.

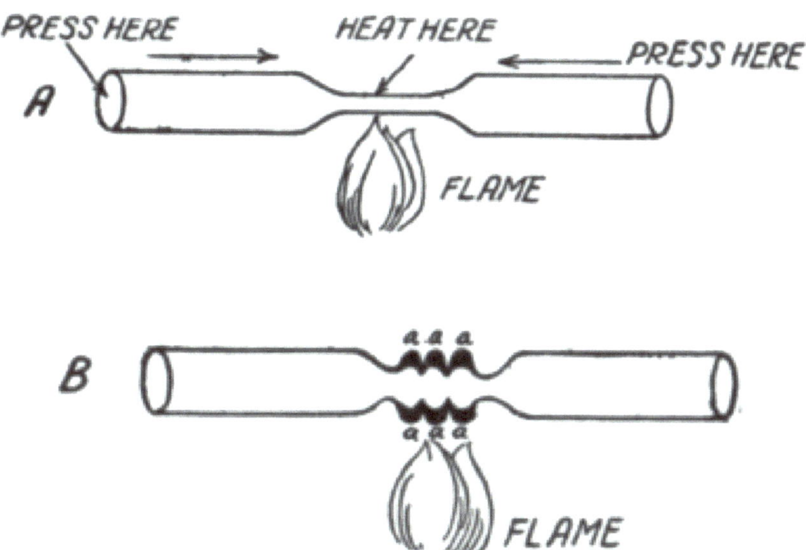

Fig. No 49 – A & B. First Steps in Blowing A Glass Bulb

Fig. 49. – A. Drawing out the tube.

Fig. 49 B. – Forming glass rings on the tube

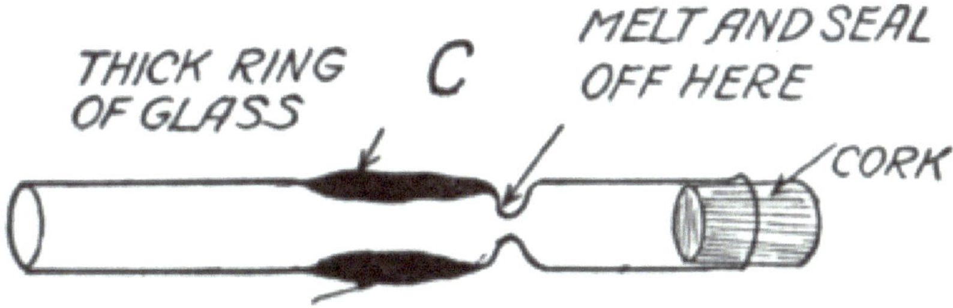

Fig. No 49 C – Making A Thick Ring Of Glass

Next heat the narrower parts marked a a a a and blow gently and press gradually on the ends to make the thick rings melt and flow together into one large ring of thick glass as shown at Fig. No 49. C: and in doing so be mighty careful that the walls do not cave in.

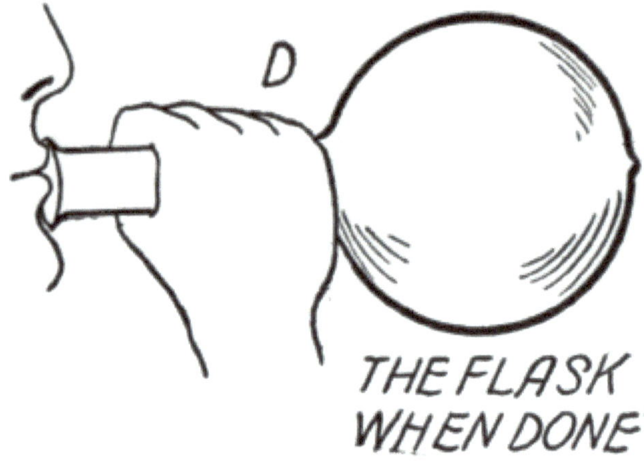

Fig. No 49 D – Last Step in Blowing A Glass Bulb

Now melt and seal off the tail and heat the whole bulb in as large a flame as you can get and at the same time turn the tube till the rings run together. At this instant take it from the flame and, still turning it, blow into it with a few little quick blasts until you get the size and shape you want as shown at Fig. No 49 D.

Reference

1. https://ie.pinterest.com/pin/209839663864026954/

2. https://www.thehistoryblog.com/archives/33823

3. https://www.science.org/doi/10.1126/science.1110466

4. https://www.alamy.com/prehistoric-manbronze-age-smelting-image151887875.html https://www.nbcnews.com/id/wbna8221331

5. https://www.alamy.com/stock-photo/iron-age.html?blackwhite=1&sortBy=relevant

6. https://www.britannica.com/technology/printing-press

7. https://science.howstuffworks.com/innovation/inventions/who-invented-the-first-gun.htm

8. https://zingerart.in/home-decorative-items/scented-candles/kota-zinger-decor-maroon-blue-white-combo-mini-pillar-candle-multi-color-set-of-3/

9. https://auradecor.co.in/products/flameless-smokeless-flickering-electric-led-tea-light-candles

10. https://www.etsy.com/in-en/listing/456386786/275-set-of-12-white-or-ivory-floating

11. https://www.radliving.in/collections/roomtype_bedroom/products/noor-set-of-2-votive-candles?variant=40843274158238

12. https://littlecreekcandles.com/

13. https://www.candletech.com/candle-making/tips-and-tricks/safe-containers/

14. https://www.quora.com/How-do-I-prepare-a-beetroot-lip-balm-without-chemicals

15. https://in.pinterest.com/

16. https://www.etsy.com/in-en/listing/1119676603/fresh-cut-watermelon-body-lotion

17. https://www.stoneyriversoap.com/products/copy-of-bath-bombs-2-5-in-diameter

18. https://en.wikipedia.org/wiki/Stained_glass

19. https://www.popularmechanics.com/home/a26289680/how-to-cut-glass/

20. https://www.istockphoto.com/photos/lavender-bath-balls

21. www://Lavender-Non-Alcoholic-Room-Spray

22. https://www.reverewareparts.com/the-etching-of-glasses-in-the-dishwasher-and-what-to-do-about-it/

23. http://www.ilpi.com/glassblowing/tutorial_bends.html

24. The Golden book of chemistry experiments, Robert Brent, Golden press New york, edition 1960.

9 798889 498588 6